L/R
GARDEN

3^{50}

D1491364

NOL

Gardeners' Lore

Gardeners' Lore

Plantings, Potions, and Practical Wisdom

MAUREEN & BRIDGET BOLAND

THE ECCO PRESS

First published as *Old Wives' Lore for Gardeners*
(1976) and *Gardener's Magic* (1977)
by Farrar, Straus and Giroux, Inc.

THE ECCO PRESS
100 West Broad Street
Hopewell, New Jersey 08525

Printed in the United States of America

The decorations have been chosen from a number of
sources including the 1521 and 1533 editions of the
Hortus Sanitatis; Gerard's *Herball* (1597); and Thomas
Bewick (b. 1753) and his school.

Library of Congress Cataloging-in-Publication Data

Boland, Maureen.
[Old wives' lore for gardeners]
Gardener's lore : plantings, potions, and practical
wisdom / Maureen & Bridget Boland.—1st Ecco ed.
p.   cm.
Combined reprint of two works. First work
originally published: Old wives' lore for gardeners /
Maureen & Bridget Boland. London : Bodley Head,
1976. 2nd work originally published: Gardener's
magic and other old wives' lore / Bridget Boland.
London : Bodley Head, 1977.
Includes index.
ISBN 0-88001-570-5
1. Gardens—Folklore. 2. Plants—Folklore. I. Boland,
Bridget. II. Boland, Bridget. Gardener's magic and
other old wives' lore. III. Title.
GR895.B66 1998
398.24´2—dc21   97-15022

9 8 7 6 5 4 3 2 1

FIRST ECCO EDITION, 1998

CONTENTS

FOREWORD

We are not Old Wives ourselves, being in fact old
spinsters; nor are we professional gardeners in
any sense. We collected the tips in this book because we needed them. Our garden for some
forty years had been at the basement level of our
house in Pimlico. It was pitch dark, and the soil
was the heavy clay of the reclaimed marshland
once belonging to Westminster Abbey half a mile
away. Gerard in his Herbal speaks of water lilies
growing there, and a very old botanist whom we
knew as children used to talk of gathering rare
marsh flowers as a boy on the site of our house.
We learned by trial and a great deal of error what
could be grown there, and from studying books

that recommended plants that would flourish in damp shade. So many of these were poisonous that we once contemplated going into business as market gardeners to supply would-be murderers who hesitated to sign chemists' registers for their needs. We then lived for a few years in South Kensington, where we laboured with more success at street level in a back garden twenty feet by twenty, which we opened by request to the public in aid of the District Nurses Fund, and which was much admired. It was even photographed for two books and several magazines—but really only because we had placed arch-shaped full-length mirrors in the back wall, giving the idea of two gardens for the price of one to many Londoners.

We then moved to our present house in Hampshire, working a garden in recently-cleared woodland on a light sandy soil on a steep hillside facing due south in a little suntrap of a valley, where the little learning we had acquired by gardening on Thames mud mostly in the dark was a dead loss. Needing to learn fast, we pestered everyone we met in the district for advice on what grew well locally and how to care for it; and we found that we were beginning to amass a store of curious information. We began to ask all our friends, wherever they lived, for the sort of lore their grandmothers had passed down to them. Modern scientific gardening books we read, of course; but we found in old books too so much practical advice of the grandmotherly kind that the new books never covered that we decided to pass it all on to those who are not afraid of finding a certain amount of superstition mingled with good sense.

—Maureen and Bridget Boland

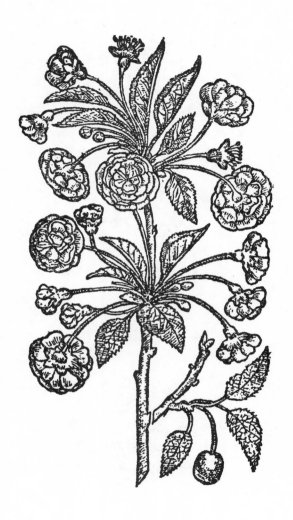

PART ONE

Plantings and Practical Wisdom

PLANTING

Consider the Moon

Every Old Wife will tell you to sow seed and to transplant only with a waxing, never a waning moon. The scientists have now caught up with this, discovering the effects of lunar rhythms on the earth's magnetic field which in turn affect growth. They have established that all water everywhere, including that inside the tiniest living organism, moves in tides like the sea. The moon also affects the earth's atmosphere so that statistically it is more likely to rain heavily (just as you would like immediately after planting) immediately after a full or a new moon. They say that a potato grown at constant levels of heat and light under laboratory conditions will still show a growth rhythm that reflects the lunar pattern. The Old Wife, without laboratory conditions or statistical tables, learned from experience how best to get her plants off to a good start.

Sow seed generously

One for the rook, one for the crow,
One to die and one to grow.

Sartorial

It is curious how often in old herbals we are advised to sow not only when the moon is full but naked, ourselves, at the time. 'The best husbandmen', writes one, 'would have the seedsman of turnips or rapes to be naked when he sows them, and in sowing to protest that this which he doth is for himself and his neighbours.' Presumably, it was hoped that the gods might look more kindly on the naked, innocent amateur than on the prosperous market gardener. Perhaps, though, the advice was not always given for purely magical reasons: we should not sow when the ground is too cold for the good of the seed, and are less likely to do so if we are told we must be naked when we do it. We have heard that in Lincolnshire, to test whether the soil was in the right condition for sowing barley, farmers used to take off their trousers and sit on the ground: if it was comfortable for them it would be comfortable for the barley. With the greater density of population, the modern gardener will probably be content to test the soil with a bared elbow, as a mother does the water for her baby's bath.

Mattresses for Beans

It was not actually an Old Wife who told us to put hair in the bottom of a trench when planting beans, but a hairdresser who abandoned his salon to go round the countryside doing the hair of invalids and elderly pensioners in their own homes. His only regret for his salon is that nowadays, working alone, he can collect less hair.

Country buses are excellent places for meeting Old Wives, and when one of us passed this tip on to her neighbour on one she said that her grandmother used to tease out old horsehair mattresses for this purpose, and also to use the results of grooming her dog and cats, as well as herself and her children. Noxious little creatures in the soil, she said, would become entangled in it, and the horsehair was strong and sharp enough to prick them to death. Anyone who as a child with bare legs has sat on a horsehair sofa can well believe this; but scientists have also now discovered that hair is full of valuable mineral and chemical properties, supplying trace elements not otherwise easily available.

Sowing Beans

Candlemas Day stick beans in the clay,
Throw candle and candlestick right away.

The second part of this admonition may not have been magical so much as economical in intent: the thrifty Old Wife perhaps considered that by 2nd February one should not need candle-light to get up by, dinner would have been eaten at three o'clock, the evening stew, already prepared, could be eaten by firelight, and one should go to bed early and certainly not read in bed.

Roll seeds of beans and peas in paraffin to deter mice.

Planting Herbs

Never plant the same kind of herb in the same place twice in succession, said an eighteenth-century herbalist, replacing a 'hot' herb with a 'cool' one—a sound rule-of-thumb for rotation that will prevent exhausting the soil of the particular properties one plant or the other needs.

(6)

Planting Cabbages

Twist a spiral of narrow tinfoil round the roots of a young cabbage plant to inhibit the larvae of the cabbage fly.

On the surface lay a piece of creosoted string or a narrow ring of creosoted felt four inches away round the plant to repel attack.

Planting Carrots

Crumble mothballs and mix them with the soil against the larvae of carrot fly. This has proved a sovereign remedy where the fly is otherwise rife.

Laying a length of tarred or creosoted string on the surface between the rows two inches from the plants has also been recommended if the former precaution has been neglected.

Planting Mint

The mixing of bonfire ash with the soil, often recommended when planting other herbs, can be fatal to mint, and should not be used even as a mulch.

Planting Garlic

The savour of your garlic, an old herbalist says, will be sweeter (whatever that may mean) if you crush the cloves a little before planting to bruise them, and also if you set olive stones among them.

Dripping for Roses

Our own most valuable, original discovery as Old Wives was made, as surely most must have been, by mistake. The over-enthusiastic use of detergents when they first became available caused the grease in washing-up water, suspended in the bubbles, to form gradually a thick cake of fat under the manhole cover outside the kitchen window. We lifted it out, but this was in London when food rationing was still in force after the War, when the throwing in the dustbin of what looked like a mass of edible dripping, eighteen inches by twelve and at least two inches thick, was unthinkable. We buried it darkly at dead of night in the back garden—not far, as it chanced, from the roots of a climbing rose which had never done very well. That year the rose flowered stunningly, and it flourished ever after. We never planted a rose again without burying fat below it, begging extra from the surprised butcher.

When we moved to the country we continued, the first year, the same practice. Every single one of our beautiful new roses was instantly dug up by the foxes that abound in the neighbouring woods, and we have had to desist. For townsfolk, however, or those with walled gardens, it cannot be too highly recommended.

Planting Strawberries

For strawberries, and only for strawberries, incorporate scrapings of topsoil from below pines and spruces when planting, and thereafter mulch with pine and spruce needles, crushed fircones and even twigs; this is said to improve the flavour.

If there are such trees near the house, you will find that needles lodge among tiles and are washed down into the gutters. The labour of clearing them is rewarded if there is a use (apart from the merely negative one of unblocked drainpipes) for the product.

Transplanting out of season

When for some reason it is necessary to transplant at a time of year when it is really too cold, puddle the plants in using hot water instead of cold. This, surprisingly, really does not damage the roots.

Bracken for Fuchsias

In the light soil of our warm and sheltered little valley we leave even tender fuchsias outdoors all the winter, so far without disaster, but we always cover them with mounds of bracken against the frosts. An Old Wife seeing this one autumn was shocked. She said that there was nothing better to dig in under fuchsias when planting them than chopped green bracken, which would encourage the roots to go down; but that they had such a passion for it that they would tend towards the surface if bracken was laid there, suffering accordingly in a hot, dry season. We now compromise, supplying bracken to both ends.

LIKES

In so unscientific a work as this, we hesitate to use the word symbiosis, which is the one that serious people now employ when writing of plants that get on well together. Older gardeners found out by trial and error what grew well in proximity and what did not without realising that they were using the Bio-Dynamic Method, happily ignorant of the nature of root excretions and the activity of organic compounds. Now that such knowledge is available, and in a form digestible by the unscientifically minded as well as by experts, no one should plan the layout of flower or kitchen garden without reference to a little handbook called *Companion Plants*, by Helen Philbrick and Richard B. Gregg (published by Watkins). Only the laws of copyright prevent us copying out large sections from it, and we have had reluctantly to limit ourselves here to such information as we have gleaned for ourselves elsewhere.

Marigolds with everything

When we were children, we spent every summer in a little house in a fishing village in northern France, which we rented from M and

Mme Noël. They lived there all the year round, retreating to a corner of the house when we arrived but continuing to keep up the garden, the only one in the village. They grew vegetables only for the house, but they sold the flowers. There was a bell that jangled when anyone came through the door in the high garden wall, and shy young men used to put a cautious hand up to clutch it as they slipped in, lest the horrible little Bolands, lying in wait, should gossip all round the village that they were courting. On the feasts of saints that were the name-days of the most popular girls, half-stifled clatterings of the bell could be heard at intervals all day long. The

village was built on pure sea sand, but inside our little walled garden the soil was as rich as chocolate. Everything grew. M Noël's particular pride were the dahlias that he bred, as big as soup plates, planted near the outside privy. It was not a beautiful garden, for flowers of each kind grew rigidly in commercially practical rows, and there were for our taste far too many of the 'everlasting' flowers in great demand for taking to the cemetery; but nowhere, surely, were plants ever so healthy or blooms so big. We learned the French names of flowers before we knew the English ones, and were much surprised when we found that what we knew as Indian Buttonholes were called in England French marigolds, but then supposed that it was because the French, as witness M Noël, had such an insensate passion for them. Every bed in the garden was edged with a miniature hedge of them, and the large beds had rows of them down the middle as well. Asked, since the scent was not attractive, why he grew so many of them, M Noël replied: 'They're good for everything.' Since he also grew many plants out of which Mme Noël made the loathsome tisanes she would try to make anyone drink who was ill, we supposed the marigolds were specifics against all the evils that the flesh is heir to; but in fact the health he was concerned with was that of his plants. Both the aroma and the excretions from the roots are invaluable, whether in flower or vegetable garden or in the greenhouse. We have since seen them often as edging plants in cottage gardens in England, and do not suppose that the cottagers, any more than M Noël, were aware that what they did was to kill nematodes in the soil, as well as whitefly. Potatoes and tomatoes need them badly.

Tagetes minuta is even more potent than the French (*Tagetes patula*) or the African marigold; and there must have been wise Old Wives in ancient Mexico, where it was sacred to the goddess of agriculture.

Nettles within reason

Nettles can hardly be allowed to rampage all over the garden, but in fact they stimulate the growth of all plants in their neighbourhood while actually growing, as well as being the best thing in the world to hasten the decomposing of a compost heap while providing it with rich ingredients. In the kitchen garden it is advised to grow controlled clumps of them, particularly between currant bushes, which will thereby fruit better and be more resistant to disease; and nothing is better when taking in a new area for any soft fruit than to use an old nettle-bed that has enriched its own soil for many years with its own compost. It is a great relief to the overworked gardener, when someone spots a nettle that in fact is not meant to be there, to be able to say, in mummerset dialect, 'Ee, now, dinna thee move thon, thon be excreting nitrogen, silica, iron, protein, phosphates, formic acid and other mineral salts, thon be.'

Doctor Foxglove

Where old cottage gardens still survive, plants that over many years have been found to grow well together will be seen still doing so in what to the suburban-trained eye will seem a terrible muddle. When carriage lamps appear on either side of the cottage door and one of those gardens fit for the ideal home is laid out, among the first things to go on the bonfire (not even the compost heap) are the ordinary old purple foxgloves with which the whole place will have been dotted. Yet the cottager's old wife could have told the newcomers there is nothing to stimulate growth and help disease resistance like the common foxglove. Apart from keeping plants healthier, they will improve the storage qualities of such things as potatoes, tomatoes and apples grown near them.

Doctor Camomile

Old gardeners used to use camomile like a visiting physician: planted beside a delicate or ailing plant for a short while it would improve its health immensely, and such herbs as mint would develop far more savour. But after a while (in fact when the clump of camomile grew too large), as though the patient had become over-dependent on the doctor and tiresomely hypochondriac, it would weaken again. The solution was to remove the camomile when it had done its work, leaving improved soil behind it in the vicinity of the plant that had been strengthened, only to replace it with a new young plant a good while later if necessary. The 'sweet breath thereof', or, as the scientists would say, the exhalation from the leaves, was considered as beneficial to neighbouring plants as it was pleasant to humans when trodden underfoot, so that camomile paths in herb gardens were particularly recommended; but this would seem to contradict the warning that not too much of it should be grown for too long in the vicinity of some plants. It is held to be entirely good for cabbages in any quantity and, if planted a yard or so apart, for onions.

Herbs outside the herb garden

Apart from the fact that growing pot herbs near the house is practical for the housewife, there is something mediaeval in the idea of a garden of herbs growing all together that appeals to most of us, as though at any time we might surprise there lords and ladies strolling 'richly dight', or a virgin sitting by the sundial or the fountain with a unicorn, its head upon her lap. But if we take the advice of Old Wives we must also grow some of our herbs elsewhere, for the good of other plants. Strawberries are particularly helped by borage, and sage, mint, thyme and rosemary are good for cabbages.

It is lucky that parsley is so decorative, for it encourages bees all over the garden, and in cottage gardens, those models of good sense that look so haphazard, it is often grown as an edging plant alternating with sweet alyssum where the suburban gardener will grow the lobelia. It is particularly valuable grown among roses, where it increases their scent, and (though you will not need it for this purpose if you plant garlic as you should—*see page* 29) it helps to repel greenfly. It is good for tomatoes, and also for asparagus.

Vegetables that make good neighbours

Since lists of which goes well with what make complicated reading (carrots, peas, beans, leeks and turnips all agree well, for instance, but of these only carrots should be planted near onions and garlic), a table would seem the simplest thing to follow. It should be pointed out that in many

PLANT	HELPFUL	HARMFUL
1 Asparagus	11 W	
2 Beans	4 5 8 10 12 W	7
3 Cabbage family	X Y	7 10 Z
4 Carrots	2 5 6 7 8 12 W	
5 Leeks	2 4 8 12	
6 Lettuce	4 10	
7 Onions, Garlic	4	2 3 10
8 Peas	2 4 5 12 X	7
9 Potatoes	2 10 X	11 Y
10 Strawberries	2 6	3
11 Tomatoes	1 W X	9
12 Turnips	2 4 5 W	
W Parsley		
X Marigolds		
Y Rosemary, mint, thyme, camomile	z Rue	

cases it is not that A is particularly good for B, but that B is particularly good for A (parsley, for instance, doing more for asparagus than asparagus does for parsley), but this need not concern us when planting them near together. That some things actively dislike each other is perhaps more important than that others do each other good. We have added to the vegetables in the table certain other plants which are helpful or otherwise to them.

Lest you rue the day

Apart from being bad for cabbages, rue is bad for many herbs. Some Old Wives say that it can make sage planted near it positively poisonous; but it is more likely simply to kill it, as it may basil.

Many people plant gladioli in the vegetable garden, simply because the stakes that they need look ugly in the flower beds. They are, however, extremely bad for peas and beans, and so bad for strawberries that these will suffer from them planted up to fifty feet away.

Ash trees

The ash has always been considered to have magical properties. Whatever its virtues for witches and warlocks, honest Old Wives would have you never plant it in the garden. They say that it is so greedy it takes all the good out of the ground for many yards around it.

We have had two curious experiences with it. We had grown a rose for some time up an old tree at the top of a slope, and it was finally brought down by the wind. A good distance down the slope grew a young mountain ash whose upper branches now came high enough for us to arch the rose across the slope to grow through them, making, we hoped, a splendid natural rose arch. Every single branch of the rose died back to exactly the point where it first touched the ash.

On another occasion, short of some pea-sticks from more suitable trees we used ash. The sweet peas we were trying to grow on them absolutely refused to cling, the tendrils we tried to wind round them uncoiling at once.

Remember, however, if you decide to fell an ash already growing in the garden, that all old country people would warn you to ask its permission first. How it will signify its assent we do not know. Perhaps the civility of asking is all that is required. It makes splendid firewood, and there are several versions of an old rhyme about how long to keep different kinds of wood before burning them, all of which end:

But ash new or ash old
Is fit for a queen with a crown of gold.

Oak and Walnut

'If an oak be set near unto a walnut tree it will not live.' This we have on the authority of a translation of Pliny by Philemon Holland, Doctor of Physicke, 1601, and alas it is not clear from this version whether it is the oak or the walnut that will die. We have not, by some mischance, the Latin by us; but frankly we doubt whether we should achieve any more specific agreement of the pronoun than the good Doctor's.

Laurels

Even if it cannot be said to belong strictly in this section, we cannot resist passing on the information that the growing of one shrub at least is good for people growing in its vicinity. Friar Bartholomew hath it that 'the land that beareth the laurel tree is safe from lightning both in field and house'.

CONTROLLING WEEDS

You need not have Couch Grass

In an area badly infested with couch we sowed
turnip seed thickly, as we were advised. We now
have no couch. You may not want turnips (and,
sown so lavishly, you will not get very large ones
anyway), but you certainly don't want couch. We
have since heard lupins and tomatoes recommended for the same purpose, but have had no
need to try them.

Ground Ivy, Horsetail,
Ground Elder

It is said that marigolds, particularly the
Mexican variety *tagetes minuta*, will control these
weeds. It may be disconcerting to the visitor to
see a dense crop of marigolds blazing in some

unsuitable part of the garden, but if this remedy works as effectively as turnips against couch who cares?

Give them excess of it

The growth of perennial weeds, particularly of a fleshy kind, can be discouraged by allowing them to grow happily till just about to flower and then harvesting them and laying them back again thickly on the surface over the roots. If you have two areas infested, lay all that you have cut on one area first, and the treatment there is the more likely to be effective. You can even search out patches of the same weed in waste ground and harvest that for the purpose.

CONTROLLING DISEASES

Hang Mothballs on your Peach tree

We carefully sprayed our peach against leaf curl, and still the leaves curled. 'Pick off the affected leaves,' said an Old Wife, 'and hang a few mothballs about on the tree.' No more leaf curl that year, though until then we seemed to be spending most of our time picking off affected leaves

and spraying with this and that. Finding ordinary mothballs at one time hard to get we tried Mothax rings; they proved equally effective and much easier to hang. To guard against a reputation for eccentricity, the reason for decorating a peach like a Christmas tree with white balls or pretty mauve rings should be explained to visitors.

Meths

Any methylated spirits that can be spared should be used to spray sprouts and cabbages against mildew.

Clubroot

Bury a stick of rhubarb here and there in the bed when planting cabbages, against clubroot.

PESTS

Step on it

A member of the panel of the BBC's admirable Gardeners' Question Time programme, speaking of identifying small creatures in the garden, said that as a lad he was told: 'If it moves slowly enough, step on it; if it doesn't, leave it—it'll probably kill something else.'

Never spray against Greenfly

There is a giant conspiracy between the insecticide manufacturers and writers on gardening to encourage the public to spend fortunes and waste hours spraying their roses against aphids.

A single clove of garlic planted beside each rose is guaranteed by the present writers (who have not been bought by the lobby—though perhaps only because they have never been approached) absolutely to keep greenfly from the plant. The roots will take up from the soil a substance from the garlic inimical to greenfly, and if in early spring a few hatch out from eggs of parents careless of their offspring's welfare they will neither lay nor survive themselves. Whatever it is that the rose takes up from the garlic does not affect its own scent, and so long as the garlic is not allowed to flower there will be no odour of garlic in the garden. Try it for one year with one group of roses in one bed protected only by garlic, spraying all the others in the garden as much as you need, and you will never waste money or time again. All members of the onion family, including chives, are partially effective, but garlic is the only completely efficient answer, the systemic insecticide to end all others. In very dry weather, water the garlic so that the excretions from its roots will be sure to be taken up by the thirsty rose.

Woolly Aphis and Whitefly

Nasturtiums are said to be your answer to aphids on fruit trees, growing the long trailing kind wound up the trunks; and also against white-fly in the greenhouse. If the latter is true it must be because of exhalation rather than of emanation from the roots, since most greenhouse plants are grown in pots and the Old Wives do not suggest growing a nasturtium in every one.

Ants

Our ancestors were more anti-ant than we are, blaming them for much of the damage done by aphids. 'If,' writes an old herbalist, 'you stamp lupins (which are to be had at the Apothecaries) and therewith rub round the bottom or lower part of any tree, no ants or pismires will go up and touch the same tree.' [I started to look up 'pismire' in the dictionary, to provide a scholarly footnote, but decided that I would sooner retain my own fantasy image of a fabulous monster like those in a mediaeval bestiary, all the more terrible for being only an eighth of an inch long. Then, a sense of academic duty prevailing, I did look it up; and all it said was 'ant'. B.B.]

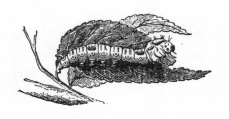

Caterpillars

Robert Ball, a Member of the Royal Society, wrote at length to the gardener Richard Bradley in 1718 about how all noxious pests, notably caterpillars, were borne in great clouds on the east wind, originating in Tartary. Windbreaks of trees, high hedges and wattle fences should therefore be placed to protect the whole garden or particular plants from that side, for no caterpillars would be found to the west of them.

Earwigs

The same Mr Bradley advised hanging 'Hoggshoofs, the Bowls of Tobacco-Pipes and Lobsterclaws on the tops of sticks' among plants 'and killing the vermin that lodge in them every morning'.

Slugs

Richard Bradley 'learned from a curious gentleman in Hertfordshire' of the efficacy of wrapping the trunk of a fruit tree with two or there strands of horsehair 'so full of stubs and straggling Points of the Hair that neither a slug nor a snail can pass over them without wounding themselves to Death'. For wall-grown trees he recommended nailing the horsehair rope to the wall completely outlining the tree; for espaliers, winding one strand round the bottom of the stem and one round the bottom of each stake. For cauliflowers a rope should be laid all round the bed.

A shortage of horsehair ropes in this degenerate age need not induce despair: an admirable trap may be made with a little beer in a jam jar laid on its side.

FAUNA AMONG
THE FLORA

Deer

In a woodland district, the only sure way to keep deer out of a garden is to build a wall nine feet high all round it, or a solid wooden paling whose

upkeep would cost more in the long run than the outlay on a wall. The rugosa rose Alba will grow to seven feet high and make in time a dense, impenetrable hedge; but if deer can jump nine feet high what is their long jump record? One remembers the stag in *The Lady of the Lake*: 'With one brave bound the copse he cleared'. Anyway, rugosas will not grow well under trees, and our garden in places blends into the surrounding woods; to erect a paling in these sections would be a sin. After we had lived here a short while we realised that we could never sacrifice the sight of the deer, at sunrise and at dusk, passing through the garden and pausing to drink at stream or pond; but all the young shoots of our roses were nibbled off. We planted enormous tree-climbing varieties like Himalayan musk and Kiftsgate which will grow to thirty or forty feet, and protected their lower stems with chicken wire while they were young, and such huge shrub roses as Nevada, whose lower, outside shoots alone suffered. We read that sprinkling lion manure would terrify the deer, and could well believe it; but then keeping the lions to provide the manure would terrify us (though we also read that lion skins would make another useful by-product, for wrapping clothes in them would infallibly keep out moths).

Then an Old Wife provided a much easier solution. Tie an old piece of thick cloth such as flannel on the end of a bamboo cane and dunk it in creosote, and stick it in the ground like a little flag near each rose, or at each corner of a bed. The deer will not risk coming near the strong smell, which will prevent them scenting the approach of danger. After a day or so the smell will not be apparent to humans unless they actually sniff the cloth. The flags should be re-dipped at intervals during the summer if there is heavy rain. The scent of violets will (in humans, too) have the effect of temporarily paralysing the olfactory nerve after a few moments, but their flowering season is not long enough to serve instead of creosote to protect your roses.

Birds

Alarmed at the expense of wire netting for our fruit cage, we used nylon netting. The squirrels sat on the crossbars gnawing neat holes, through which so many birds entered that we soon seemed to be keeping an aviary rather than a fruit cage.

We reverted to the Old Wives' practice of winding threads of black cotton about among the fruit; the birds have difficulty judging the distance of such threads against the sky and fear entangling their wings if they have to take off in a hurry. It is, at any rate, a deterrent. Nylon thread will not snap when branches are blown about in the wind, or when (undeterred) birds do blunder into it.

One Old Wife has proved that primulas and yellow crocus, elsewhere ruined by birds, are left untouched growing beside a lavender hedge. We propose to grow lavender among our soft fruit, at any rate along the back of a strawberry bed; it will do no harm to try it, but we shall watch the growth and flavour of the berries compared with others grown elsewhere, for strawberries are kittle cattle and may dislike the proximity of so strong a herb.

Moles

Small lumps of acetylene fuel put down the runs are effective, the damp in the soil activating them; but they should be stored in a really airtight container. We had kept some in a damp shed in a too loosely-covered jar; it was greyish instead of black when we used it, and we found a new hill the next day in the place where we had just removed the old one, with the fuel, now white, cheerfully crumbled among the freshly turned earth of the new run.

Gerard, the sixteenth-century herbalist, advises the placing of garlic in the mouth of a mole's run, 'and you shall see him run out, astonied'.

We did, and we waited, and we didn't. Perhaps we did not wait long enough.

The growing of caper spurge in the garden is also recommended as a deterrent; we grow caper spurge, and it may deter some, but living on the edge of woodland we have so many moles that unless the whole garden was full of nothing but caper spurge it is unlikely that it would deter them all.

But if molehills you have, use the beautifully crumbled soil, mixed with sand, for potting.

Cats

An Old Wife, troubled with neighbours' cats that rolled on her catmint and lay sunning themselves on her favourite alpines, wrote to a national newspaper that she had discovered a cure: lay a length of the inner tube of a bicycle tire on the lawn, and the cats will think it a snake and give the garden a wide berth.

Wild Cats

If you are troubled with these, it is said that they 'will flee from the smoke of rue and bitter almonds'.

Flower-Arrangers

'Shee that would have posies is a sore tryall to the good Husbandman of his Garden,' as some old herbalist might well have said, except that the vice of flower-arranging is a comparatively modern one. Admittedly much of the space in old gardens must have been taken up with the growing of 'strewing herbs' for mixing with the straw that preceded carpets, both for sweet scents and for aromas that deterred mice, fleas and lice. But it was the Dutch flower-painters who (largely, we suspect, to encourage the sale of Dutch bulbs in the 'tulipomania' period) popularised the notion of massing mixed flowers in vases. The Japanese, who create masterpieces with three twigs, must be far less unpopular with their gardeners. The flower-arranger who is not a gardener should never be let loose with a knife or scissors out of doors, particularly near shrubs. Since mantraps are now illegal, the best way to ensure that anything is left flowering in the garden at all is to see to it that such flowers as are brought into the house last long there before they need replacing.

All flowers will last longer in water if foxgloves are incorporated in the arrangement. If their presence is not considered suitable for a particular artistic effect, add foxglove tea to the water: pour boiling water on a handful of leaves and flowers, or leaves alone if the flowers are not in season, and allow them to steep overnight. Put pennies in the water. For delphiniums and larkspur, add sugar; for daffodils and narcissi, add charcoal or camphor. Put the cut ends of chrysanthemums in very hot water for a moment and then straight into very cold. Wrap the stalks of tulips as soon as they are cut in newspaper and stand them for several hours up to their necks in water. Daffodils (which excrete a substance poisonous to other flowers and the handling of whose stems even gives some people a rash) should preferably not be mixed with anything else in a vase, but if the arranger insists see that they are soaked first for an hour in separate water and then rinsed again. Topmost buds should be nipped from delphiniums, gladioli and snap-dragons.

Heathers will last for weeks in the house without the flowers withering or the needles dropping off if they are kept without water—a fact which is particularly useful with the winter and early spring flowering varieties. Forsythia and winter-sweet will last longer if picked in bud and stood first in hot water than if picked already in flower. If flowering shrubs must be used, not just the flowering tips should be cut but the whole of the flowering shoot down to two buds above the old wood.

WASTE NOT

Kitchen refuse

Anything you can eat plants can use too. Even caviar could no doubt be added to fishmeal with good effect. The outer leaves of vegetables need not even be composted but can be used as green manure, either chopped up fine and dug into the lower spit of soil when planting or into the top spit several months before any planting is to be done there. The contents of the sink basket should go on the compost heap, with the caveat that meat scraped from plates should be excluded: foxes, and even some dogs, will scatter the whole heap about if they smell it. One peculiarity that we cannot explain is that, although coffee grounds scattered on the heap in the ordinary way seemed of no interest to animals, grounds thrown there in the little paper cones used in Melitta coffee filters were always carefully extracted and the paper, cleaned out, scattered far and wide. We blamed the foxes on general principle. We had the impression that they said to each other: 'Let's go up to the farm for a chicken dinner and then down to the Bolands for coffee,' but a zoologist tells us we imagined the whole thing.

Tea-leaves

Old Wives, when they have finished telling fortunes, save their tea-leaves to put as a mulch on camellias, which benefit particularly from them.

Milk

When milk bottles are to be rinsed they should first be filled with water and well shaken, and the contents used as a very mild liquid manure on houseplants and in the garden. Climbers planted against house walls always tend to get too dry. and luckily for the housewife she need not go far from the kitchen to find a useful place to rinse out her bottles.

Soapy water

Before the days of detergents, Old Wives recommended the throwing away of soapy water, particularly if it had soda in it, on flower and vegetable beds, saying that cabbages benefited particularly. People who, like us, have septic tanks and should not use detergents can at least be grateful for this by-product of their labours.

Banana skins

Laid just below the surface of the soil, banana skins have long been said to be very good for roses, and scientists now approve the practice, having found that they are able to provide, as they rot quickly, a considerable quantity of calcium, magnesium, sulphur, phosphates, sodium and silica.

Beer

Charlie, whom we meet on our country bus when we go shopping, tells us that he once threw what was left after brewing home-made beer out of his kitchen window. There was a row of hollyhocks just outside, and, while the rest of the row did reasonably well, the hollyhock immediately below the window grew to a height of eighteen foot six inches, 'and a man from the BBC came down to see it'. Rinse out your beer bottles and glasses, like your milk bottles, for the good of the garden. It is in this case, apparently, the yeast that does the trick.

Boots

Never throw old boots and shoes in the dustbin, but bury them in the garden. Leather is full of good things, and they will rot down eventually, except for loathsome rubber and plastic soles which can then be retrieved. The salts in human sweat are not without their uses, either.

Egg boxes

Do not give your egg boxes back to the grocer or milkman, far less throw them away: they are just as good for growing small seedlings as peat pots, and cost you nothing.

Old Nylons

Nylon stockings are strong enough and have enough give in them to make perfect tree ties.

A Use for Horsetail

Gerard says that horsetail was known also as pewterwort, and that it was used for scouring pewter dishes and wooden implements in the kitchen. It can also be used for cleaning aluminium if you run out of wirewool. Make a little stubby two-ended brush about three inches long by binding a bunch of the stems with two pieces of string about half an inch apart. Both the sides and ends of this can be used. If, as is to be hoped, you have eliminated it from the garden, look for it growing wild in damp places. If an aluminium saucepan has been burnt, first boil an onion in it and pour off the scum that will rise.

WEATHER

In these days of weather-forecasting satellites, old methods may be despised; but meteorological offices only give us a very broad general picture, and old people in the district should always be listened to for ways of foretelling local conditions. On our summer holidays in France as children we always knew that it was going to rain next day if we could see distinctly the white cliffs of the Kentish coast across that narrowest reach of the Channel; and from a certain flat in Rome the same could be said if you could pick out actual houses on the distant slopes of the Alban hills.

In *The Country Calender or the Shepherd of Banbury's Rules*, of the late seventeenth century, there is a pleasing variant, given in three languages, of the old adage 'Red sky at night, Shepherd's delight, Red in the morning, Shepherd's warning'. It gives us a pleasing picture of the pilgrim trudging across Europe in older times: 'In England,' writes the author, John Claridge,

> *A red evening and a grey morning*
> *Sets the Pilgrim a Walking.*

In *French* thus:

> *Le rouge Soir, & blanc Matin,*
> *Font rejouir le Pèlerin.*

The *Italians* say the same:

> *Sera rosa, & nigro Matino,*
> *Allegro il Peregrino.*

He also quotes an English proverb:

> *In the Decay of the Moon,*
> *A cloudy Morning bodes a fair Afternoon.*

Again:

> *When Clouds appear like Rocks and Towers,*
> *The Earth's refreshed by frequent Showers.*

He says that his own observation has confirmed the saying that a general mist before sunrise near the full moon denotes fair weather for a fortnight; if this is seen in the new moon, there will be wet weather in the last fortnight as it grows old; but he warns us not to predict from the first night of the new moon but from a couple of nights later.

In hot weather, when the wind has been southerly for two or three days, he says, and clouds are piled like towers one on another with black on the nether side, there will be thunder and rain suddenly; and if two such castles arise one on either hand, it is time to take shelter hastily. If clouds 'look dusky, or of a tarnish silver colour, and move very slowly, it is a Sign of Hail, which if there be a Mixture of Blue in the Clouds will be small, but if very yellow, large.' Above all things, he advises us, watch the bees, for if it is going to rain they will not leave the hives, or fly only short distances from them.

We make no apology for quoting proverbs, for, as Bacon said, 'they are the philosophy of the common people'. Here is a versified collection of many of them from *The New Book of Knowledge*, published in 1758:

> *If ducks and drakes their wings do flutter high,*
> *Or tender colts upon their backs do lie ;*
> *If sheep do bleat or play and skip about,*
> *Or swine hide by straw bearing on their snout ;*
> *If oxen lick themselves against the hair,*
> *Or grazing kine to feed apace appear ;*
> *If cattle bellow, gazing from below,*
> *Or if dogs' entrails rumble to and fro ;*
> *If doves and pigeons in the evening come*

Later than usual to their dovehouse home ;
If crows and daws do oft themselves bewet,
Or ants and pismires home apace do get ;
If in the dust hens do their pinions shake,
Or by their flocking a great number make ;
If swallows fly upon the water low,
Or woodlice seem in armies for to go ;
If flies or gnats or fleas infest and bite,
Or sting more than their wont by day and night ;
If toads hie home or frogs do croak amain,
Or peacocks cry—soon after look for rain.

Mouffet, in the seventeenth-century *Theatre of Insects*, observes that 'if gnats at sunset do play up and down in open air, they presage heat; but if they altogether sting those that pass by, then cold weather and much rain'. They will help you, he says, to find water in times of drought, where, after sunrise, 'they whirl round in an obelisk'.

Dry weather

However foretold, when the dry weather comes we must water. Sages advise us to water only in the mornings between mid-September and May; even when watering-in new plants, it should not be done late in the day lest, icy at night, it damage the roots.

We read that when planting a peach you should sink a pipe an inch and a half or more in diameter and a couple of feet long upright alongside it, with its top just above the surface, and water into this in hot weather, to encourage the roots to go down and to supply them with enough moisture there. As we grow several huge roses such as Kiftsgate and Himalayan musk up trees we set such pipes down alongside them, for they have to be planted close to the trunks of the trees where the soil tends to be always dry. Although properly speaking, of course, water from a butt should always be used, this is a slow process if one has to stand by the quickly-filling and slowly-emptying pipe with a can; so in a long dry season we confess, we turn on the hose, put the end down the pipe, and leave it slowly trickling for as much as a quarter of an hour; and, at any rate, on a steep sandy hillside we have roses growing thirty feet high after five years, doing well, and bidding fair to grow another ten feet or so.

The gardener of a palazzo in Rome, responsible for the staggering display of plants in the great earthenware containers on the terraces,

amazed us by saying that he only watered them twice a week even in the height of summer. Each container had two or three holes at the bottom of the front surface; these would be stopped with bungs, and the container watered till two inches of water stood on the surface of the soil for quarter of an hour; then the bungs would be taken out. Any tendency for the soil to leach out was combated by frequent top dressing with mulches, and the removal of some of the soil every autumn and digging in quantities of manure—usually a mixture of sheep dung and a leaf-and-bark compost. Certainly huge azaleas and oleanders flourished under this treatment as well as geraniums, plumbago, and such; but even fuchsias did not suffer from it.

Cold weather

When frost is expected, plants in need of protection should, to our surprise, be sprayed with cold water in the evening, which will generate enough heat in evaporating to prevent frost damage.

After a hot, dry summer, the bracken, so useful to cover plants with against frost, tends to have very little substance and after a few weeks to have shrivelled almost away. At such times the top-hamper of Michaelmas daisies can be cut back as soon as flowering is over and used for the same purpose; piled cross-hatched it will give almost as good cover, and is practically indestructible, as anyone will know who has been foolish enough to include it in the compost heap.

PART TWO

Gardener's Magic

When my sister and I were sifting material for our book on Old Wives' Lore we had reluctantly to put aside a lot that we hated not to pass on but had to admit did not fulfil the requirement that we had set ourselves, that the advice should be practical, however eccentric. I have drawn on that surplus for this part of the book, which is really as much about gardeners as gardening; for gardener's magic is about the hopes and fears of men, in love or loveless, terrified or inquisitive, always in trouble of some kind or other, who looked out into the garden for help—and perhaps found it, because they were so sure it must be there.

—Bridget Boland

FOR LOVE

Food for Lovers

The Doctrine of Signs (that every plant bears some mark of the use to which it can be put) is very important in gardener's magic. 'Behold', says Paracelsus, 'the Satyrion root, is it not formed like the male privy parts?' No one can deny this. Accordingly magic discovered that it can restore a man's virility and passion. The lupin and carrot were, though to a lesser degree, considered aphrodisiac for the same reason, as were Shakespeare's 'long purples', that botanists call *orchis mas* but 'liberal shepherds give a grosser name'.

'Periwynkle when it is beate to a poudr with worms of ye earth wrapped about it and with an herbe called houslyke,' says an early translation of a Book of Secrets attributed to Albertus Magnus, 'induces love between a man and his wife if it be used in their meals.' As so often with magic one wonders how the strange virtue of these humble ingredients in combination came to be discovered. The difficulty of wrapping a worm round some powder would seem considerable; but the great Albert was probably no cook. The ingredients are easily grown, the houseleeks on roof tiles or in any crack or cranny in a wall, and periwinkles in any shady corner, particularly if it is a little damp.

In the same shady corner can be grown sowbread (*cyclamen napoletanum*), sometimes found in wild woodland and easily made happy with a little leafmould. Gerard says that 'Sowbread, being beaten and made up into trochisches, or little flat cakes, is reported to be a good amorous medicine to make one in love, if it be inwardly taken.' That splendid Renaissance lady, Caterina Sforza, who captured castles and held Cesare Borgia at bay and knew as much about love as war, held that sowbread did wonders for a woman's looks—which may explain the efficacy of the other recipe as well. Culpeper, in the seventeenth century, maintained that the roots of *asparagus saturis*, boiled in wine and 'taken fasting several mornings together, stirreth up bodily lust in man or woman, whatever some have written to the contrary.'

'Our gallants' "sweet powder",' writes Evelyn, is made chiefly of 'the white and dotard (decaying) part' of the ash. The white dead nettle, whose leaves are delicious cooked in butter, was thought lucky for lovers (if not aphrodisiac) because in the flower, if you hold it upside down, the stamens can be seen lying for all the world like two people side by side in a curtained bed—whence its name Adam-and-Eve.

Love Potions

The spreading of Islamic culture in the middle ages, particularly after the coming of the Moors to Spain, brought much Arabian magic to Europe and from as far away as Persia, including a potion to make one in love. It was compounded of cloves, laurel seeds, Italian thistle and sparrow-wort, drunk in pigeon broth. The Arabs also recommended the annointing of the male member with pyrethrum and ginger in lilac ointment, and the female parts with balm of Judea.

Spring water in which willow seeds have been steeped was strongly recommended in England as an aphrodisiac, but with the caveat that he who drinks it will have no sons and only barren daughters.

The Lovers' Bedchamber

A bridal bedchamber, we are advised, should first be fumigated with burning leaves and fruit of the bramble as a magic protection against any evil wished upon the couple by disappointed rivals.

The fumigation should be performed well in advance, for the windows of course must not be opened lest the virtues of the smoke drift out, and the odour of burning brambles is not of the pleasantest. This would have been counteracted in older times by the strewing of sweet-smelling herbs on the rushes on the floor, those considered best for the bridal chamber being verbena, marjoram and meadowsweet, mint, thyme, valerian and violet, all sacred to Venus, and basil and broom, sacred to Mars. A bowl of pot-pourri containing them could be placed on a table by the door instead. It should be stirred, we are told, with the fourth finger of the left hand by anyone coming in, to release the scents and induce the mood of love.

The sheets of lovers should be perfumed with marjoram—Virgil says that when Venus carried

off Ascanius to the groves of Idalin she laid him on a bed of it, and she should know.

Pillows stuffed with verbena were recommended for their strong aphrodisiac scent; but strong is the word, and a sprig of it thrust in among the down of the modern pillow might well suffice.

At the bedhead should be hung, that surest of all talismans for lovers, a piece of mandrake root. The mandrake's roots derived their magical properties from the Doctrine of Signs, for it resembles the human form; but it grows wild only in eastern Mediterranean countries, and was difficult and expensive to obtain. Those who wanted the talisman were therefore warned to beware of substitutes, for roots of the native bryony could, with a little adaptation, be made to resemble it and were often sold at fairs as the real thing. Lovers were also warned not to take powdered mandrake roots internally, for it has a narcotic quality (indeed, too much of it can send one to sleep for ever), and even a little of it will induce a drowsiness which will defeat its purpose in the bridal chamber.

When we remember that beds were canopied and curtained against the draughts, the couple with their scented sheets and pillows and their talismans would be cosily prepared for love indeed.

Precautions

Understandably, perhaps, when all marriages were 'arranged' and the attentions of the spouse must often have been singularly unwelcome, mediaeval herbalists were much concerned to provide anti-aphrodisiacs as well. Hildegard of Bingen, a twelfth-century nun, gives counter-potions against the effects of the mandrake, of which she passionately disapproves. One involves picking seven shoots of broom and the roots and leaves of one cranesbill and two mallows, which were then pressed and rubbed and mashed (using the middle finger only) in a mortar till they formed a paste that could be spread on a cloth and bound to the body, which would nullify the power of the mandrake completely.

Arabian herbalists advise as anti-aphrodisiacs a decoction of henna flowers, or of onions with egg-yolk and camel's milk, or of chick peas and honey.

Other magical herbs apparently had more permanent effects: a woman who drank salvia cooked in wine would never conceive; nor would she if she ate a bee.

When infidelity is suspected, we are assured, certain precautions can be taken against the lovers by the spouse. Plutarch says that white reeds, picked just before sunrise in a river, and strewn in the wife's bedroom, will drive the

adulterer mad and make him confess. Male chauvinist that he was, he evidently took it for granted that the wife would be the erring partner. To keep a wife from erring when he is away, Arnold of Villanova (early in the fourteenth century) advises the husband to hide two halves of an acorn in the pillow (as was done by magicians hired by defeated rivals to inhibit conjugal love). But he kindly adds that the lovers can counteract the long-term effects at any rate of this by putting, if they can find them, the two halves together, keeping them for six days, and then eating half each.

When love, who laughs at locksmiths, has made a mockery of magic too, and even the most careful of spouses fear themselves deceived, the mandrake is summoned to the rescue again. It is then that a mild decoction of the powdered root might save the breaking heart with a night's oblivion. Shakespeare doubted it. The Moors in his day were credited with knowing more of magic than anyone, and Desdemona's father, for one, certainly believed that Othello had won her love 'with some mixtures powerful o'er the blood' or other occult arts. But once the seed of doubt of her fidelity is planted in Othello's brain, Iago can safely whisper as he watches him:

> *'Not poppy nor mandragora*
> *Nor all the drowsy syrups of the world*
> *Shall ever medicine thee to that sweet sleep*
> *Which thou ow'dst yesterday.'*

TO PROTECT THE GARDEN

If a garden always expresses in some way the mind and spirit of the gardener, is it too fanciful to believe that something of the peace we find in old gardens comes from steps that its makers took to ensure it? Every care was taken to see that no evil should enter. The summoning of dark forces for our own purposes is all very well, but no one wants the occult blowing about where it listeth out of control.

Occasionally on entering a very old walled garden you will see over the door a horse's head carved in stone. This is the relic of a belief that dates from Roman times. 'Some have used to put in the garden the skull of a mare or she-ass that hath been covered,' wrote Topsell in 1607, 'with the persuasion that the garden will be fruitful,' and Pliny was even of the opinion that it also kept out the caterpillars. A 'physic garden' would sometimes have carved over the door the ancient sign for secrecy, an open rose with two buds above it, to preserve the secrets of the herbalist's art.

In the crevices of walls houseleeks were encouraged, to protect the garden's luck and also to keep out lightning.

If in digging deep the modern gardener

should turn up a very old earthen pot, it may mean that someone took the advice of Pliny, and buried a toad in it against storms and hail.

The ancients planted the laurel against lightning—a sure protection, the thirteenth-century Bartholomew assures us. If the laurel is found darkening the house, however, it is more likely to have been planted by Victorians to prevent the neighbours looking in or, like an uncle of mine in Ireland, to prevent the servants wasting their time watching people playing tennis in the garden. To credit trees with magical powers seems pleasanter.

The trees themselves were felt to need protection too. A good Christian monk, the thirteenth-century Abbot of Beauvais, advised the hanging of coral in an apple tree to defend it against all weathers. Probably one of the little pieces that form a natural cross would have been his choice. Others suggest that when the apple is planted the name of Asmodeus, the devil who tempted Eve (unless you believe it was the she-devil, Lilith), should be written on the earth and cancelled with a cross. Cider used to be poured over the roots of apples as a libation and the poet Herrick records the custom of drinking to the health of all fruit trees on Christmas Eve:

> '*For more or less fruits they will bring*
> *As you give them wassailing.*'

On the oak, sacred tree of the Druids, the Celtic sign of the circle divided into four equal parts used to be carved for protection (lest it fall), long after Druidic worship had been forgotten.

In the same way some old-fashioned gardeners will still always grow a certain plant 'for luck', having forgotten the original significance of the magic: verbena, for instance, that was held by the Saxons to be a sure protection against storms and hail, as the ninth-century Leechbook of Bald and Cild assures us.

Animals in the Garden

Those wise in witchcraft would never allow a parti-coloured animal in the garden, such as a tabby cat or a black-and-white dog. This tabu probably derives from Genesis XXX and XXXI, in which parti-coloured animals are regarded as unclean. The modern gardener may find it easier to ask his neighbour to keep his dog or cat under better control by claiming such a superstitious view as this and getting a reputation for mere eccentricity, than by saying the creature is badly trained, and being considered offensive. The tabu did not apply to birds, luckily, except the magpie, which does rather flaunt its challenge.

Those who had beehives were advised to hang juniper inside them against adverse magic, and to 'rub all within with fennel, hyssop and tyme flowers, and also the stone on which the hive shall stand' (Gervase Markham), for this will make the bees 'love their hive and come gladly home'. This is an admirable example of the giving of magical significance to a piece of sound common sense, for the scouring of the hives with these herbs will clean them and also scent them with herbs that bees do indeed seek out. Bees, by the way, should always be paid for, for while stolen plants (particularly in the case of rue) are said to thrive best, this is not true of bees. And if you are much stung by them do not complain too loudly, for they are known to sting fornicators most.

The owner of a dovecote or pigeon loft was advised to be sure to hang in it the head of a wolf, so that 'neither cats, weasels nor anything that will hurt will enter' (Lupton). As with so much magic, the modern would-be practitioner may find this prescription difficult to follow. Perhaps a fox's mask would do instead.

When Walking in the Garden

It was regarded by French herbalists as unlucky (but fortunately rare) to see an aloe in flower. Except in the evening, when it was fortunate, it was unlucky to see a spider, as it was to see a squirrel at any time. If you saw a spider spinning, it meant that someone was plotting against you. If you saw a cuckoo while it was actually singing, you would be, had been, or were being cuckolded.

Gerard is very specific about what can be divined from oakapples, which 'broken into at the time of their withering, do foreshadow the sequence of the year' to Kentish husbandmen. 'If

they find an ant, they foretell plenty of grain to
ensue; if a spider, then, say they, we shall have a
pestilence among men; if a white worm or a mag-
got, then they prognosticate a murrain of beasts
and cattle.' Lupton goes further: 'If the little
worm doth fly away, it signifies wars; if it creep, it
betokens scarceness of harvest; if it turn about,
then it foreshadows the plague.'

It has always been considered safe to savour the
odours of the garden on the air as you walk, for
plants that have evil in them hold it close while
they grow; but it was said that you should not on
any account lie down to rest under an ivy tree and
fall asleep, for it could be the death of you.

WORK
IN THE GARDEN

In the Toolshed

The ancients advised that yarrow should always be kept hanging in the toolshed 'for safety'; and it came to be believed that the plant protected the shed from entry by thieves. Here is an admirable example of the good sense often hidden in magic: yarrow staunches bleeding—in France it is known as 'the carpenter's herb'. What better reason could there be for keeping a bunch of it hanging handy in a toolshed? The ancients also advised that it should be bound round the handles of tools for work outside.

When helping in other people's gardens we are sometimes puzzled by the presence of very strange equipment in their toolsheds. I have often been asked the purpose in mine of a piece of bent wire from an old coat hanger on the end of a long pole. It has in fact no more sinister use than exactly fitting my gutters so that I can stroll round the cottage scraping, with no trouble, leaves and pine needles from them.

The magically-minded would keep among their tools the longest possible iron nail, as only an iron nail would serve for digging up certain roots for magical purposes, and it could be a tedious process with a small one. But frequently tools, especially knives, made *without* iron were called for; presumably this dated from very ancient times when iron was regarded as a new-fangled thing and rather vulgar, much as we look upon plastics now, while flint was still respected.

A gold knife or sickle absolutely had to be kept for cutting mistletoe. A bull's horn and a bone were other tools that could be kept for digging when iron must not be used.

Many of these tools have, of course, perfectly practical uses. I realised recently, when trying, without unpicking half a rockery, to move without damaging the roots a plant that had grown too big, that a nicely curved bull's horn was exactly the tool I needed to poke under stones with, and that my toolshed was inadequately equipped.

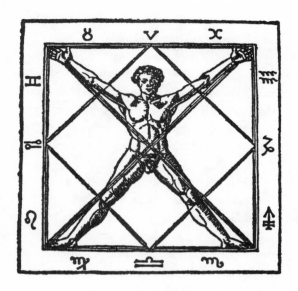

At Work

Great attention has always been paid by gardeners to the phases of the moon; and this not only because it affects the plants but because man himself is wiser (according to Michael Scot in the thirteenth century) when the moon is waxing, and therefore any work that needs thought, such as planning a layout, should be done then. Attention must also be paid to the zodiac, whether sowing, planting or picking a herb, confining the work if possible under a sign auspicious to the plant. Vervain (*verbena officinalis*) for instance, is peculiarly sacred to Venus, as to some degree are any plants used in love potions and the like, and therefore the position of planets needed, it was felt, sometimes to be considered.

All repetitive actions in the garden were better done nine or seven times, or in multiples of these numbers, which are magical in the oldest lore; three has only been magical since the coming of Christianity, as representing the Trinity, and in Christian magic nine is regarded as three times three.

When a plant to be grown is of particular importance, such as the mandrake, the soil thrown up by moles, ants or beetles should be used in preparing the position, or that which lies between cart ruts. It need not trouble the enthusiast in magic that the latter injunction may have originated in someone realising that soil between cart ruts had probably been well manured. For growing plants for love-potions, particularly valuable, according to Pliny, was the soil taken from under the print of your right foot wherever you were standing when you heard the first cuckoo of the year—especially for would-be adulterers, perhaps.

Whoever practised garden magic, whether professionally or for personal use, would find that stocks were constantly being depleted by the demand for roots at inconvenient times of year. All roots that are used in magic, however, can be dried; and presumably the professionals kept a stock, cleaned and carefully labelled. If a client failed to pay for a root, the gardener would replant a portion at once in the same place; for the client's trouble would then continue to grow worse until the cash was handed over.

Sowing Seed

Watching the phases of the moon has always been regarded as particularly important when sowing, which should only be done when it is waxing, not waning. This ordinance is now known to be scientifically justified, but I confess to a sentimental attachment to the notion that the forces involved are magical. Even if the moon has now been danced on by astronauts and is littered with American Space Authority hardware, over my garden (and surely yours too) she still shines enchantment. Besides, the sceptical reader should beware: you never know when the wise men of today may not catch up with the magi.

Certain seeds, the ancients felt, need special care in relation to the moon. 'Mark,' says Holinshed's version of Pliny, 'how many days old the moon was when the first snow fell the winter next before, for if a man do sow rapes and turnips within the aforesaid compass of that time, the moon being so many days old, they will come to be wondrous great and increase exceedingly.' During the twelve years I lived in Rome it only snowed once, and the inhabitants of the City spent their time tobogganning on trays down the steps of the American Embassy; but this is a degenerate age.

Parsley must absolutely be grown from seed, and never, never moved about. Everyone agrees about this. Elinor Sinclair Rhode, in *Herbs and Herb Gardening*, quotes a French saying: '*Repiquer le persil, repiquer sa femme.*' She also quotes old sayings on the difficulty of growing it even from seed: it is so slow to germinate because it goes back nine times to the devil. But if you sow on Good Friday you can prevent this. Never take a house with an established garden in which parsley is not growing, or you will never see the year out. The trouble for the previous owner may have been, of course, the fact that it takes an honest man to grow parsley; or he may have been aware that he who grows it well will have no sons and only barren daughters. All round, it seems safer for a man to make his wife sow it; and indeed there is another saying that where it grows well it is the man of the house who wears the trousers.

Cummin seed is apparently particularly bloody-minded, for when you sow it you should ram it down hard and adjure it not to come up; which it then will.

For Picking

Before picking or digging up, the plant should always be 'saluted' and told for what purpose it is needed, and if possible for whom, thus pacifying it and ensuring its co-operation. Modern investigators who claim that the reactions of plants to being manhandled, or even spoken to harshly, can be scientifically registered, would probably agree that this is a wise precaution. You should spit three times on the piece you pick, and it must never be allowed to touch the ground. There seems to be a feeling that a piece picked off the ground is like carrion, unholy, with the virtue gone out of it. You should never face into the wind as you pick, or look back over your shoulder at the plant after you have done so.

When a plant is to be picked by hand we are warned that it is usually better, and sometimes essential, to do so with the left hand, sometimes even with the thumb and fourth finger of the left hand—the stronger the magic in a plant the fussier it is liable to be. A sixth-century manuscript advises you to hold a mirror over a herb before picking it, before sunrise under a waning moon; you should also be chaste, ungirded, barefoot, and wearing no ring. Modern advice for picking blooms for a flower show is always to do so before the sun is on them, but for magical purposes it is nearly always enjoined that the sun should not have risen at all. In the case of picking from a peony or digging up its root this is absolutely vital, says Pliny, or the woodpecker of Mars is liable to pluck out your eyes.

Some plants require more elaborate rituals than others for their virtues to operate. Thus to use camellia to cure cataract all you need to do is to pick it before sunrise, telling it that you need it 'for the white growth of the eyes'; but for senecio to be effective against toothache you must dig up the root without using iron, touch the tooth with it three times, and then replant it at once; luckily this can be done in daylight, so that it is not necessary for both patient and gardener to be up in the small hours. When picking mistletoe the time does not matter (which is just as well, as it may be difficult enough to climb the tree without having to do so in the dark); but you must sacrifice two bulls beneath first, use your golden knife or sickle, and drop the mistletoe down onto a white cloak stretched out below.

We pick lettuces more often, in the ordinary way, than mistletoe, and probably all too often omit the essential rite of making the sign of the cross over them as we do so. In a book by St Gregory the Great said to have been translated by King Alfred (two surely very reputable authorities) there is a salutary warning about this. A maidservant working in a monastery garden did so, and became possessed by the devil that had been in it. When exorcised, the devil complained that it had been merely 'sitting on the lettuce and she came and ate me'.

The Mandrake

The most elaborate precautions of all have to be taken when digging up the mandrake root; but first a word on how it grows. Too many people think it is as mythical as the phoenix, but its botanical name is *mandragora officinarum var. vernalis* and it can be found wild from Greece, all round the eastern end of the Mediterranean and North Africa, to Spain. The illustrations of it in ancient herbals tend to have been drawn, like those of the rhinoceros or the camel in bestiaries of the same period, by artists who had never actually seen it. In reality it grows like a big rosette almost flat on the ground, with long leaves and very short-stemmed, bluish-purple, cup-shaped, sweet-smelling flowers. The fruits that follow the flowers, and nestle in the heart of the rosette, are yellow and about the size and consistency of a small tomato, unpleasing to the

average palate, but evidently an acquirable taste as the local children are said to enjoy it even to excess, when it causes dilation of the pupils and headache. They normally spit out the seeds, which if swallowed can cause temporary madness followed by catatonic sleep, but are not fatal. The seeds and powdered root were much used in early medicine as an opiate, and by those with Borgia-like tendencies as a poison (though it must have been difficult to administer, not being the sort of thing that could be described as 'tasteless in tea' or, to anyone with an educated palate, in wine). But its chief commercial value seems always to have been as a talisman.

The root does go down exceedingly deep, certainly as much as five feet. The Greeks believed that you might even, if you fell into the hole when you had dug it up, tumble straight down to Hades. Usually we are advised to draw a circle on the ground around it, and some experts prefer the use of ivory or the horn of a bull for this. Some say that the ground should be soaked at intervals for three months with hydromel (one part honey to eighteen parts water, boiled) to 'appease the earth'. Conceivably this may make the operation easier, but the root has now to be dug out without the use of any iron tool. Infinite care must be used not to damage it for it must emerge in the recognisable shape of a man or a woman, and the actual removal should be at sunset. If it is not tugged too violently at the last, it will not give the terrible scream that turns men to stone; but you are advised to tie a dog to the upper part as you lift it so that the evil will go into the dog. Some authorities require elaborate incantations, but others hold that 'In the name of the Lord God of Sabaoth' is enough. The hole should then be filled with sweet fruits or nothing will ever grow there again, which would be a pity for, given its natural habitat, it will have demanded a choice spot in the garden with a full southerly aspect, preferably in a light, sandy soil, for ease of extraction. The root should be treated with every respect and kept wrapped in a shroud, for some say it is the true Origin of the Species of mankind. Paracelsus denies this, but thinks it is not unlikely that a man, or at least an homunculus, may yet be bred from it.

FOR THE GARDENER

Not only the garden but the gardener himself was seen by those who practised the magic arts as needing protection, perhaps even more than other men, for he who has skill will have rivals, and he who has power will have enemies. Luckily he did not need to be constantly drinking potions or rubbing on salves for protection, since many herbs were considered effective if just worn or carried about.

An amulet against evil spirits conjured by others could be made of cloth (preferably red) filled with dried betony, peony, and artemisia. Herb bennet was so powerful that 'Satan can do nothing and flies from it', and, as a bonus, the *Hortus Sanitatis*, 1491, says that 'if a man carries the root about with him no venomous beast can touch him'; but I do not know if this is valid for fornicators in the vicinity of beehives, and fear it may only apply to serpents, basilisks, and such.

Dried in a sachet, or even worn as a flower in the buttonhole, the periwinkle (known as Sorcerer's Violet) was by common consent sovereign against any witch not carrying it herself who might come visiting.

A useful string of beads could be made as a charm against all forms of evil out of dried peony roots; they might be carved and fashioned as you would (to make them look innocently decorative), but should not be dyed or painted except with the blue of woad or the yellow of meadow saffron, both protective plants themselves, or the virtue will be sealed in.

The superstitious gardener of today may care to consider the value of ancient advice when he goes out beyond the safety of the protected garden. Hang a root of rhododendron round your neck to preserve you from any savage dogs you may meet. If you are going out to dinner, take some syderica with you as a sure protection from all poisons, particularly (since it bears the image of a serpent on each leaf as a sign) that drawn from snakes.

The surest protection against drunkenness is to wear a wreath of ivy. A woman, of course, if she wishes to conceal that she has any problem in this respect, can always hide the wreath with her tiara. A man can take the alternative precaution of eating five bitter almonds before the meal, which Pliny assures us is effective, and a Roman of his period should know.

Alyssum will prevent anyone getting angry with you, and if you carry heliotrope you can be sure to hear only friendly words spoken. The latter should be wrapped in a laurel leaf with the tooth of a wolf; it should only be picked when the sun is in Leo in August for this purpose, but it can be dried. At a party you expect to enjoy, however, it might be an embarrassment, since no fornicator present will be able to leave until it is removed and you may feel obliged, in common courtesy, to be the first to leave yourself.

To Give Special Powers

Both Bartholomew and the good Bishop Vincent of Beauvais testified that a decoction of heliotrope, drunk with the invocation of powerful enough spirits, had the power to give invisibility at will.

Sometimes invisibility might, apparently, be found not to be enough, and the adept would need to take the form of some other kind of life, and then, to get back into human shape, to bathe in spring water into which anise seed and a laurel leaf had been dropped; if this was not altogether effective (perhaps some trace of the animal form had remained, such as cloven hooves), a strong decoction of the same plants should be drunk.

If the adept, or indeed anyone else, had taken the outward form of an ass, all that was necessary was to eat roses (only the old alba, gallica, centi-folia and damask varieties can have been meant when this was written). Perhaps to this day if a donkey is seen eating roses it should, in charity, be left to do so, and not be driven off until it is quite clear that it is *only* a donkey.

For powers of divination, vervain has always been regarded as sovereign. The Romans used it in all lot-casting and prophecy. Heliotrope was also thought helpful for all forms of divination, and today might be particularly useful if the gardener's burglar alarm should fail; for he has only, according to Albertus Magnus, to sleep with it under his pillow to dream a reconstruction of the burglary, complete with recognisable burglar. 'And,' says the rhyme of 'Robin Goodfellow' (1628), albeit with his tongue in his cheek,

> *'Can a magician a fortune divine*
> *Without lilly, germander, and sops-in-wine?'*

Before we mock the superstitions of the past, we should consider some of the preoccupations of our own time. To acquire the ability to see ghosts the Society for Psychical Research should note, carry lavender. It has certainly the most memory-evocative of all scents, and when a garden or room is heavy with it even the least sensitive may feel that round the next corner, or at a turn of the head, anyone who has trod these paths before or crossed this floor might well be seen.

The power to see fairies is more difficult to acquire. They are not at the bottom of every garden. Wild thyme must first be picked 'on the side of a hill where fairies use to be.' The word is 'use', note well, not 'used', so make sure the tradition of their presence is a living one. The injunction comes from a recipe of 1660, which

recommends that you take 'a pint of sallet oyle and put it into a vial glasse; first wash it with rose-water and marygolde; the flowers to be gathered towards the east. Wash it until the oyle becomes white, then put it into the glasse, then put thereto the budds of holly hockes, flower of marygolde, the flowers on tops of the wild thyme, the budds of young hazels. Then take the grasse of a fairy throne [ant hill], then all these put into the oyle in the glasse and sett it to disolve three days in the sunne and then keep it for the use.'

FOR A MERRY HEART

There are in the old herbals innumerable recipes
for what are nowadays called 'heart conditions'
(as though the healthy heart were in no condition
at all); but there are also many less strictly
medical, for the heart as the seat of all our
emotions. Is it a hark-back to such ancient magic
when pills to calm our anxieties are marketed as
Purple Hearts?

Borage provides without doubt the most
popular magical herb for the heart. Pliny says it
should be called Euphrosinum, so surely does it
make a man merry and joyful, and Gerard that,
drunk in wine, it makes 'men and women glad
and merry, driving away all sadness and dullness'.
The modern cocktail-party host who decorates
tall glasses of this and that with sprigs of borage
surely has no idea how old a practice he indulges
in to ensure the success of the evening. Gerard

quotes an old saying in dog-Latin which he translates as

> '*I, Borage,*
> *Bring always courage.*'

Like several other herbalists, he also recommended balm and basil drunk in wine.

For the older writers the effects of these herbs seemed purely magical; Paracelsus, on the borderline, considered balm the basis of the Elixir of Life; by Gerard's time medical explanations were beginning to emerge; and it is now understood that balm is an excellent nerve tonic (cheering the

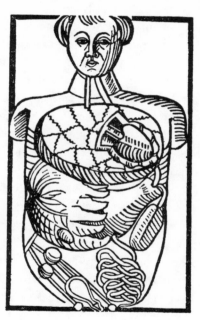

heart indeed). Basil is an even better choice to be taken with alcohol if the party is liable to prove a long one, for it is not only that rare thing, a nerve tonic that is stimulant rather than sedative, but it also settles the stomach, preventing vomiting and nausea. Meadowsweet, according to Gerard, should be boiled in the wine 'to make the heart merry'; and if you make a kind of brandy by distilling the flowers of lily of the valley in it, it will not only comfort the heart but even 'restore speech to those that are fallen into the appoplexie'.

Lest the sceptical modern reader suspect that alcohol is the active ingredient, there is much magic for the heart that does not call for any. Chervil (sweet cicely) roots work wonders 'for old people that are dull and without courage', (Gerard), and marjoram boiled in water 'easeth such as are given to much sighing'. Bartholomew prescribes fumitory: he admits that is is 'an herbe with horrible savour and heavy smell', but 'is natheless most of virtue, for it cleaneth and purgeth melancholy'. You can make the heart merry with 'rosset sweetcakes' of archangel or rosemary flowers baked with sugar, which sound altogether more agreeable.

A purgation of hellebore will 'cheer the hearts of all dull and heavy persons', while one of bugloss is said to be particularly exhilarating for infants. Germander and milk thistle need only be chewed to lighten the spirits. The virtues of

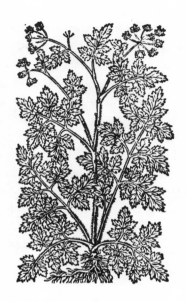

lavender seethed in water to comfort the heart are praised as far back as William Langham in 1579 and as near to our own times as Baron Frederic de Gengins Lassaraz in Paris in the 19th century, who specially recommends it for 'the nervous disorders to which ladies of high birth are subject', poor things.

Personally, I always take the advice of Shakespeare on anything, and he recommends another thistle. 'Go,' says Margaret to Beatrice in *Much Ado about Nothing*, 'get you some of this distilled carduus benedictus, and lay it to your heart. It is the only thing for a qualm.'

FOR CERTAIN PEOPLE

For the Student

You cannot start education too young, as the advocates of pre-nursery schooling aver—but they do not go back far enough: ante-natal clinics should perhaps provide quinces, for it was held in the seventeenth century that 'the woman with child that eateth many during the time of her breeding shall bring forth wise children and of good understanding'. Bugloss is as good for the infant's mind as for his heart. At school, Evelyn says that borage 'will cheer the hard student'. The memory can be vastly improved by smelling or eating rosemary or betony, which indeed are both good for the head generally. 'The flowers of lavender quilted in a cap,' says Turner's Herbal, 1551, 'comfort the brain very well.' Often in old portraits of men of letters they are shown wearing what appears to be a nightcap, and I had always presumed until I read this that it was to impress upon one how studiously they burned the midnight oil; but now I wonder if they were comforting their brains with lavender.

For Athletes

Olympic competitors should check that these aids are permitted by the Committee, but it used to be considered that of value to all athletes were baths in which were steeped mint and balm 'to strengthen the nerves and sinews'. Eating nasturtium was said 'to soften the muscles', but whether this meant to prevent stiffness or cramp or to prevent the ageing athlete becoming muscle-bound I do not know. The marathon runner should put artemisia and/or camomile in his shoes against weariness in the legs, and also carry a stick, however small, of myrtle for the same purpose. After the race the whole body can be annointed with oil made from nasturtium seeds to 'soften the muscles' again. Any runner will surely benefit from the advice of Webster in *The Devil's Law Case* to one of his characters to eat 'Malaga raisins to make him long winded'.

TO TAKE INDOORS

Against Evils

The magic of the garden, of course, could be used to protect the house as well. Some people still hang up horseshoes outside their door, a relic of the belief that witches feared cold iron; but herb bennet, the blessed, would once have been hung over it inside to keep the devil from crossing the threshold, with betony for the further good of the souls of all within.

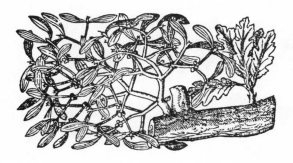

Nowadays mistletoe is brought in only for kissing time at Christmas, but once it hung in every hall all the year round as a sign that guests greeted under it were safe in that house, a recognition of its power, known from Druidic times, to ensure peace and friendship. Other beneficent herbs would be strewed over the rushes on the floors along with such more practical things as pennyroyal (*mentha pulegium*) to deter fleas. If Queen Elizabeth I were coming on a Progress, the wise householder would be careful to strew much meadowsweet, which she was known to value above all, though possibly more for its scent than for its other virtues

To protect the house against the entry of the plague, bunches of rue (herb o' grace) used to be hung at the sides of windows, particularly those facing east, for it is on this side that the infected 'air blows from France'. So powerful was it considered that thieves looting plague-contaminated houses would risk entry if they carried it even if corpses still lay there. Here again we can trace the explanation behind the magic, for though the plague was not airborne it was carried by rats, and rats hate rue.

Our ancestors used also to rub furniture with herbs. The revellers disguised as fairies in Shakespeare's *Merry Wives of Windsor*, after ordering that the elves should strew 'good luck' herbs in every room, decree

> '*The several chairs of order look you scour*
> *With juice of balm and every precious flower,*'

and this not for the scent alone; though alas modern manufacturers who add oil of lavender, probably synthetic, to wax furniture polish have probably forgotten the magic significance of what they do.

Magical Pot-Pourri

Owing to the prevalence of close-carpeting, pot-pourri is probably the most practical way for the modern magic fancier to keep dried herbs in the house, and a far more magical scent will certainly pervade the rooms than that of more conventional kinds. For instance, special bowls of herbs recommended for the bridal chamber on page 58 can be kept in all bedrooms, to which can be added plenty of sweet woodruff, which has the magical property of causing anyone who sleeps near it to dream of summer meadows and wake in a world of new-mown hay even in midwinter. I can find no specific magical use for costmary, (*chrysanthemum balsamita*), but would add it for its scent: in America it is known as Bible Flower (which perhaps sanctifies it), because it smells so sweetly when dried and lasts so long that it used to be pressed between Bible pages and kept there as a bookmarker.

There are, of course, dozens of methods for making pot-pourri, but there is one, devised when magic was taken seriously and therefore perhaps most suitable, in *Delights for Ladies* by Sir Hugh Platt of the court of Elizabeth I. It was designed for enabling you to keep the flowers whole, so that there is no need to tear the petals off and discard the calixes; but of course when, as with most of these herbs, the leaves are as scented as the flowers, they are stripped from their stems. The flowers and leaves should be laid first carefully in a box on a bed of dry sand, with more sand between each layer. Sir Hugh then left the box in the sun, avoiding moisture and cooling, but for modern purposes you may use an airing cupboard, with the door left a crack ajar to allow moisture to escape lest evil spirits create a mould; it should be left there for twenty-one or let us say three times seven days, or nine times nine if the herbs are fleshy. The flowers and leaves will be found to have kept their shape and a memory of their colour as they dried.

The method was particularly intended for roses, whose beauty alone should allow us to count them among plants that 'comfort the heart',

even though they were never thought magical. But do not use modern varieties: hybrid teas, floribundas, and hybrid musks, however sweetly they smell when growing, do not hold their scent well when dried. Best of all are the old damasks, particularly the one usually marketed as Kazanlik, from which the famous attar of roses was made; the Red Rose of Lancaster (*gallica officinalis*, the apothecaries' rose) and the red cabbage rose, centifolia, come next; China and Bourbon roses, and the rugosas (which all have a hint of cloves in their scent), are excellent. All flowers and leaves for pot-pourri should be picked in the morning, when the sun has had time just to start volatising their essential oils, say by about eleven o'clock. Fixatives, always used in modern pot-pourri mixtures, are not really essential for this magical one; but if you like, for even longer life, add (when the other ingredients are dried) to a quart of them a tablespoon of powdered orris—which you can make yourself by drying the roots of white iris germanica very thoroughly for two or three months and grinding them. It has a scent of violets.

The mixture should be placed in a glass, porcelain or earthenware bowl, but by no means in one of silver or pewter, which the plants will dislike and tarnish in their ire with some trace of the essential oils which they have retained.

ORIGINAL
CONTRIBUTION
TO MAGIC

No book of this sort should fail to include at least one addition to magic lore. In keeping with our technological age, I contribute one for starting a motor mower. It is no use swearing at the machine, or invoking any of the demons potent in herbal magic—this has been tried. Attach to the handle a piece of fennel (for flattery, see Ben Jonson, *The Case Altered*, Act II, Scene 2), and then salute it with admiring words, saying it always starts at the first tug of its cleverly-designed cord; and assure anyone within earshot that it is the best machine on the market. And this, as the herbalists say, is sovereign.

INDEX

(99)

(101)

ABOUT THE AUTHORS

The Boland sisters tended their gardens in London and Hampshire, England from the 1930s through the 1970s.